HOMUNCU1

David Greenslade

David Greenslade PhD, has lived many lives. Before working as a lighthouse keeper he was a bus conductor in the south Wales valleys. He spent three years in remote locations in Japan and then toured the USA and Canada working in native American, Amish, Quaker, Basque and Mafia communities. He has taught in Welsh medium schools and at European Universities, mentoring poets and writers as well as steering his own work through film, theatre and television. He recently taught and continued writing in the desert interior of Oman. Following a long immersion in contemporary lifestyle experiments, he currently teaches at University of Wales Institute Cardiff. He is an ordained Zen monk.

also by David Greenslade

Burning Down the Dosbarth (Y Lolfa, 1992)
Panic (Red Sharks Press, 1993)
Fishbone (Y Wasg Israddol, 1993)
Creosote (Two Rivers Press, 1996)
Yr Wyddor (Gomer Press, 1998)
March (Y Wasg Israddol, 1998)
Old Emulsion Customs (Y Wasg Israddol, 1999)
Each Broken Object (Two Rivers Press, 2000)
Weak Eros (Parthian, 2002)
Adventure Holiday (Parthian, 2007)
Zeus Amoeba (Two Rivers Press, 2009)

HOMUNCULAR MISFIT

David Greenslade

PS AVALON
Glastonbury, England

First published in the U.K. in 2011 by PS Avalon

PS Avalon
Box 1865, Glastonbury
Somerset, BA6 8YR, U.K.
www.willparfitt.com

David Greenslade asserts the moral right
to be identified as the author of this work

cover image and photo of the author:
David Rees Davies

book design: Will Parfitt

ISBN 978-0-9562162-7-4

CONTENTS

ACKNOWLEDGEMENTS

Thanks to editors of the following magazines:

*Borderlines, Poetry Salzburg Review,
Scintilla, Seventh Quarry.*

Some of these poems
previously appeared in a pamphlet,
On The Go
with illustrations by William McClure Brown
for the Beyond the Border
International Storytelling Festival,
St Donats Castle, 2004.

DEDICATION

We live in a rainbow of chaos
Paul Cezanne

Chaos is the score upon which reality is written
Henry Miller

*One must still have chaos in oneself to be able
to give birth to a dancing star.*
Friedrich Nietzsche

Chaos can be freeing
Ginette Paris

NÉE SHELL

Tried that, didn't work.
Tried again – tried anything –
abandoned when it worked.
If a project offered home I soon played
eviction order, top ten stress, inside out, sudden death,
evacuation, split bet, stretch, squeeze until
it breaks (or holds), wild horse, *cheval*, centrifuge roulette.
Camping in white mist, the grey scale
where I was born left behind
for distant rainbows beaten with foxes
driven from culverts, surrogates
that might have been me, but I was hiding
in a dimple the night sky millwheel
failed to grind, hull intact – ready for
the siege of incompatible outsider wheat.

LION IN THE SOUL

That night all the help lines were closed
I had to fight blue-tongued lions
clawing my solar plexus.

Armed with a slackrope, split-sole
slippers more like bubble shoes,
and a long drooping pole, I set about holding my own.

The rope bristled with razor wire,
balance pole salient with monkeys.

I started to prepare three hot water bottles
and turn my attention to a good night's sleep –
docile rubber shapes, triangle, circle, square.

Ghoulish scaffolding offered to embrace me –
an argent shade in the brushed steel surface of the fridge,
my blurred reflection at gaze in a black window.

I heard a voice calling – jump from this isolated billet,
become the herald of my own unwinding banner.

SOMETIMES A PANIC

Sometimes a panic lands in my belly
as delicately as the paw of a wounded tiger
and I know there's no escape.

Another time terror
is a feral cat whose persistent
whining makes me want to let it in.

The cat's dry nose so close
it baits the decoy I've been training
to drag its broken wing.

The cat could be a midwife
but the way it considers my guts,
this cat is a benevolent monster.

Monster or midwife?
I'm a garden sparrow
tormented for entertainment,

so tight with dread not even a pinhead
bereft of angels could press in. So light
with screams my back would be broken by a prayer.

SPARKY

Slowly an empty mirror kindles beauty   Mayumi Oh

We lay on a coconut mat
near a fire of chopped palettes
waiting for sparks to fly into our mouths –
nothing could harm us,
even harm became divine.
Next morning
holes in our clothes,
blisters on our cheeks,
painful giggles when we swallowed –
how we eat affects digestion –
an evening spent catching sparks
in an open mouth
is similar to catching raindrops
or swimming through a field of wheat,
it's my kind of party,
serving paradox followed by coincidence.
Why turn back at the boundary end
of infinity's mobius strip?
Leap – there's more to cosmic vanity
than a mirror filled with time.

MY CLOTHING PARADIGM WENT QUANTUM IN THE SHOPPING MALL

My clothing paradigm went quantum in the shopping mall.
Guards suggested, "Too many mirrors and
                    no time for reflection, eh?"
They knew the problem. The solution, they said,
conform to local news, respect the myths
that mould my *mabinogi* in the world.

Smiling at cleverly folded money, double or quits
financed card tricks shared in that warm cabin.
Praise a gardener's allotment for a while and eat,
otherwise avoid a widow's garden gate advice.
Blisters reimbursed the shed I burned.

One guard's eyes predict an early discharge date
but nothing leaps to beat the hole I'm in into a halo.
They comment, radiators love the knuckles of a minstrel
planning an extension to his broken heart.

A call to the police ripens all our anecdotal gifts – and,
fascinated by my own ordeal, I was ready to unwrap
one more for almost anyone.   But quarantine was boring.
The world became a language game I played
until the stories that I dealt in didn't fit.

RETREAT

Stop – this isn't a military retreat.
Troubles may be formidable, but no
one is under attack. Not even you. Disarray
is not despair and you are here to change a little
something in your mind, not the world.
That takes care of itself. No one is indispensable
nor should they feel neglected by clear sky, constant rain,
falling leaves, speeding traffic, a thousand mobile phones.

Drop your troubles at the hostel gate,
notice how differently, when you
walk along the drive or rolling in a car,
the sound of it has changed. The muddy lane
responds to something you never noticed
had this metabletic gift. Leave physical objects,
not lazy fantasies – heirlooms, letters,
photographs – everything you need to leave behind.

Abstract distractions won't keep anything away but,
like a sieve of panic, allow the least determined vermin
fragrant nests. Dump your distress where it's plain to see,
boundaries are a fabric shield where scars fade slowly into stone.
Exult in limps. Deteriorated suffering also hurts.
If you like that pain so much, you can always stuff
your shoes with thorns more loyal than your own.

Outwit familiar miseries by playing with your voice
every time you give your name and share what's up.
Don't beat others with tactical insolence,
save it for the goblins you like to share your cabin with
as you lurch around the world. At the end of your first month
you might fall asleep, not starved of problems, but with the bread
of angels doubling the torment of your borrowed hospice bed.

OTTER BOY

It's the faraway look that attracts me
more than the faraway place.
I prefer local chaos. One
by one my friends moved so far out
very few of them came back,
those that did had changed so much
we were never really friends again.

Instead of travelling myself I hung around the wake
of their departure, danced at the funeral of some
avoided the hagiography of others,
had the compliment of living in a freak show
of meandering skin walkers, assembled boundary riders,
religious hybrids, crop-weasels.

Offered another way, my own slip-free ticket,
virgin passport, foreign currency,
I returned to the glue of familiar rivers
particularly walks between Ogwr and Cynffig,
a real otter boy when it comes
to the threat of what I really want.

I occupied my mother's language
and doubled my opportunity. A chance
to wake from trance and memory,
as if no other system achieves the same,
just as a poem with its morbid snakes and exalted ladders
shifts towards the remote proximity of words.

SOVEREIGN MAGIC
ON THE SEVERN BRIDGE

I'd been paid to deliver a best man
from Thatcham to a wedding
somewhere in the Forest of Dean
but he'd forgotten where the wedding was.
He was more than drunk, insisting we stop
on the motorway for him to puke and urinate.
At last, the spell he cast caused a tyre to burst.
As I freed the heavy spare and couldn't find the socket lug
he managed to cast his pungent breakfast
well into the wind, halfway across the Severn Bridge –
both of us gale-fucked, speckled, sour above the tidal mud.
I experienced a waking nightmare
and perceived the country tearing itself apart
cleaved between Somerset and Gwent
to a soundtrack of Gloucester wedding guests all retching.
As the land beyond Chepstow blurred
into oscillating scrub, I wanted to pitch
my companion high over the mighty safety rail,
blaming our puncture on his sympathetic wreck.
But fog and rancour jogged his Forest memory
and while we were awaiting rescue, just
as he would have lunged back into the car,
flattened to the forward inside flange, he said,
"I've got it man, the nuptials are in St Briavells."
I decided to abandon this cidered paranymph
spatchcocked in the middle of his sudden neurovictory,
as chronically unbalanced as the car that carried him.

CHAKRA CLEANSING

I love these alien Sanskrit umlauts
their mutable, sea group, throat anemone,
exhaling smile mouth, choral glee balloons,
acrobatic, narrowly stretching,
exactly pursed for the tubular chime
of a sacral, aspirant, pack growl.

We discipline our workshop drones –
collectively harmonise rasping overtones,
stroking upper palettes with our tongues
as if an elephant seal, that never knew a predator,
were audibly licking drift roe from the roof kelp of a sunken cave.

It booms.

Nadis make rag puppets of our Mountains of the Moon
                                        kimono laundry,
wring their hard work, yin-yang, spring flood salt exertion
into dark pink, Orinoco, tidal water jugs.
It's an eclectic jumble sale – riff-raff bric-a-brac
with the focal depth of hardened superglue.
Our spindrift teachers can't get mainstream work
and so inflict their esoteric recovery experiments on us.

More ablauts. This time the great continental vowel
drift rumbles forward, roaring from the solar plexus.

My heartfelt, cordate, slow-release, diaphragm exhalation
side-twists wayward, hunched, tense as a bawling child,
wide, tight pulling down the corners of my lips.
My purple face exceeds the cut belly sag of a gutted trout
and I achieve the eee-squeak sphincter only dart fat perfect.

Aural windjets – apophony before epiphany –
blast shuttered pupils' star-lit apertures,
scourge the middle way's meridian reflux,
descale the cloudy mirror's temporarily non-dairy,
algae free,
lactose avoidant, triglyceride, double helix, soya milkshake,
my spectrum, all too human – frail-foil – broadcasts in.

One final warning from the shiny ponytail:
caution how we junk up
our bright clean, inner windscreen –
avoid caffeine, thoroughly chew brown rice.

But I – dear teacher, warrior, athlete, amazon,
adore my downward flights
and, instead of staying up
at dizzy heights glimpsed
in workshops, gardens and in prayers –
descend from pure sound,
spinning from each vortex to the depths
like a child whirling on pretended, helicopter wings,
spitting out the sip of nectar our chants distil
with a lust for voice that visiting
each remote, hermetic station brings.

ÜÜÜÜÜÜüüüüüëëë ë ë ïïïïïïïï . . . . . .

BLISS RISKS

Taking risks for bliss –
first round goes to sheer bewilderment,
a benign punch hurling me into a dewroll
through the labyrinth.
                              Grass blades compliment
my vulnerability to frost.
Stings sharp as papercuts
numb my balls into synaesthetic
porous spheres withdrawn
into my subtle body.

All I can think
is sacred geometry sees through me
and when I try to join the motorway
clover aimlessly through logarithmic spirals
down a quadrant of junctions – fluent in knots
but unable to capsize from the widening bight
under construction onto a proper road.

Some parts of me,
those not too stunned from rolling
on the frozen lawn, reel
while driving at the prospect
of always being diverted but never on a path
as, at sixty miles an hour, I currently am.

I thaw a route through a ripple of bollards,
the colour of dewrollers as they rise from the ground,
play the peddles like a Hammond organ,
feet pumping a holiday from Newbury to Wales.

But now, while merging
into the syntax of faster cars
something unexpected – a nag, as corrosive
as a stub eraser ferruled to a pencil habit,
allows a clutch of guarded antonyms
above the parapet to contradict me.

I'm lost on a stretch of road
I've driven a hundred times before.
The shock of rolling through the labyrinth
has blurred the circuits of my world.

GOING TO CRAZY

Going crazy on a moderate idiom,
assembling its metaphor quietly in the verb
because I don't have anywhere else 'to go' .

Good natured boobies flock to the belfry wherever I am,
screws draw water even when
I'm dry – perfectly motionless, perfectly still.

Trouble did come once when I stood
beseeching the summit of Crystal Mountain
for a path through trackless time.   I met

a creature that offered me a magic saddle,
no strings attached – just sit and ride,
but this visitor looked distinctly odd.

How could I trust a putrid benefactor
that stank so clearly *causa mortis*, a donor
unlike anyone I'd ever met before.

It had fists as thick as a Bible,
eyes hollow as pleural cavities, donkey lips,
millipede legs fluttering a march towards me.

Its broken breath, a shattered fishtank,
riddled the 'saddle' at me. Ride it (*ride it Cefn Rider*).
I answered The Crazy in several languages.

Like Hell! How could I trust a beast like that,
pouring an avalanche towards me, as if mud,
rocks, snow and broken trees were bodyguards.

We played cards. Then we played
stare-until-you-blink. Mr Crazy almost wins,
and bridle the endurance saddle reign.

But I have a conjuror's trick. Ocular dementia.
I can shift the pupils of my eyes
away from the cornea – two

black moons travelling across
alternative skies of vitreous white.
The first to blink has to pay a forfeit

of the winner's choice.
After battling a mental void
I request a more chaotic winter.

EXIT SIGN

Elbowed off the garden wall,
gouged out from the cul de sac,
angle-cut from the year I was born,
well and truly down on my luck.

Bleached out of the kitchen drawer,
scared off from the dog bowl,
plunged clean through the sewer drain,
don't show your face round here again.

Blow torched from the mantle shelf,
Kleenexed from the mirror,
lifted from the picture hook,
where I thought I'd hang forever.

Airbrushed from the photograph,
vaporized from the mezuzah,
salted from the kitchen floor,
wafted from the oven door.

Curling a tin in a quarry shed,
sharing sardines with the watchman,
we both consult the hexagrams
but our throws won't show a pattern.

EMPTY MEANING

I threw the dice,
cut the cards,
divided yarrow stalks,
chased birds around the bedroom.

A lot depended on it
and I wouldn't look elsewhere.

What the dots said,
guts pulsed,
water rippled,
tortoise shell cracked,

would be what I thought about today,
crave a distant girlfriend,
come to my senses, turn around,
make a living, fiddle my expenses.

Nothing outside the splashes,
the marks, scribbles,
tear drops and their oracle on the page.

UNCERTAIN BUT RETURNING WING

Uncertain but returning wing
remembering how a cuckoo uses all
its strength to change a nest into an arena.
I donate my brothers to the butcher,
sisters to the carnivores,
every begging bowl
I roam the world to fill,
I claim as mine.

Stretched to reach as much
as my reflection
breaks the back of a speckled mirror,
I try a birdbolt gambit
as if a bandit jackpot
could nudge my migrant soul
from sonic infamy
to a smaller cage.

I plot a course
to breach the threshold interview,
peal a chime to clarify obscure
feelings while, like a bag of steps,
I dive towards them.
First prize?   An executioner's noose
coiled from a trace of the finishing line.

ORCHARD IN THE RAIN

Silk net showers of rain drift like herring milt
onto lactating shoals of apple trees but
seem to fall no further than Joshua silhouettes
digging deeper into seven years of stubborn praise.

Prophets press their lips against the feathery squall,
withered codlins on wet black boughs blossom into shlock
titanium androids whose italic assassin fountain pens
target the Masonic foreman's double headed eagle.

The tufty Oxford lawn sprung with drizzle
flips heavy ground mist in devoted rags,
puckered volutes of recumbent water
trace a pilgrim's smock-work flag.

As the man steps clear of his own stained glass window
the barrel spring that launches him sags a terminal groan –
sand and lime poured into the bearing pitch –
a permanent gag that stops this story from ever speaking up again.

FREQUENCIES AWAY
(ON RETREAT)

I'm still an interval away
from the song I want to sing,
rehearsing lines whose zealous
pitch gets coarser. Proud cadet, agile,
adaptable, my eyes salute
the ripples of an unknown flag.
Now my current ploy
offers edifying food and drink,
wide-eyed therapeutic practice
where I invest reckless money
with gullible ease. Broke,
I climb into a fallen Yggradisil,
whose field, like a crypt,
excluded me
until maggots whistle,
prizes rot,
when the team I'm on claims victory

SLIDE PUZZLE

A plastic, slide puzzle – showing
a white unicorn with big, black eyes
on, fifteen, smooth, yellow tiles,
in a purple frame,
free with a fast food meal –
as if I could solve it.

I was meant to push
small imprisoned squares
with the tips of my fingers
and gather the scrambled picture.

No matter how
I shoved the panels, the unicorn
remained chopped up.
Its exaggerated stare gazed off.
Hooves, tufted with snowy down
side-stepped any trouble.

The long, spiral alicorn, dispersed
across three panes,
stayed
snapped.

WEST HENDRED

A place for noticing the tile
beneath my boot
might have been there
for the last five hundred years

but I was the one
blown from life
until like a straw
I landed here – again,

among stigmata, on retreat
where rampant bears
and passant lions
grab for me.

Burned, encaustic
wax pressed the clay
I scarred with more
than one appearance.

Briefer than a tile,
my frozen biovector
cracked beneath
a pattern more than mine.

CANDLE

(for Peter Spriggs)

I arrived as dull as any distraction,
only a neutral bit of me showed through
a cellophane window in a cardboard box.

Quickly inflamed, sharp as a pinprick,
the spark – flaring
just above the charcoal trace of it.

The entropy of my self-absorption
biased in a loop of wax and plasma,
culled to thirsty flat-braid candlewick.

Christening card obituary,
one small flash in a night of ice and rock,
within that light, a condensed dark echo of brilliant waste.

SERENDIPITY

I soon started to enjoy the place.
Proud of being good listeners
we heard each others' slightest cut
blossom into full fledged wounds
then eavesdrop as they festered.

My room, as clean and comfortable
as a wizard's conclave cell.
I loved retreating there and borrowed
hospice books before re-reading mine.
Found bits of tile for my windowsill.

In the kitchen I peeled, chopped,
ate all the food, cleaned my plate,
tried to avoid intense debates,
kept secrets, blood groups, bones
in other people's diets, to myself.

Something happened almost every day
one ran away, one cried, all were moved.
I was thanked for pitching in
when all I wanted was to be alone,
take long walks, read and sleep.

I followed the way things were done –
meditation, gardening, workshops,
and at almost any time – sympathy –
someone to talk to, those who scour
their own ears with other people's saga.

One day, cleaning the toilets,
I found a gold ring at the bottom
of a white ceramic bowl, as if riches (like trouble),
were offered from the least of fjords,
right under the treasure hunter's nose.

It belonged to one of the women.
I never found out how it got there
but she thanked me in her room,
then later came to mine. The salty
shelter smiled on serendipities like these.

THE GIRL WITH LOGORRHOEA

When I hear about fresh ground spices
for the fifteenth time, I grow tired of cloves
and anistar, how she ties back her hair
and then the various ways she
blends shampoo, how a supervisor
picks her battles, or stands firm;
where in the rainy street she lost it
at the end of shift, in what order
she files receipts, marks her page in books,
cleans the unchosen paintwork of her front door.
Even falling asleep, from side to side, she talks.
Bed and breakfasts can be funny,
not only tents but what goes in them, a lot,
who went where, when, waking with what
odd object inadvertently slept on.   Questions
I move too soon to answer – yes I have seen really
massive starfish, shooting stars, changed a tyre
on the motorway, roller blading in the park,
thrown a frisbee, washed an avocado stone,
unexpectedly – yes, I have shot and eaten quail.
Her spoken diary, every equal, equal detail.

SHEARING STRAIN

Travelling
and the animal can't stop,
pistons can't stop,
heart won't stop pumping,
as though something far away depends on it.

Food arrives, wool scrolls
from mountain sheep to bo peep coat hook,
zips concede and fortify my rucksack,
fine sand minimises the computer screen,
maximises the distant guest house,
a call to the answerphone – *I miss you.*

The body is still a soft machine
that likes to be smoothed with lavender oil,
praised for a good night's sleep,
that likes to swim in the lake,
speckle toast with lavabread,
get kissed at the party.

I check the instruments to see what time it is,
where I'm meant to be, who with,
how fast I'm going, in what direction,
the ingredients of my drink are puzzling,
I'm thirsty like I've never known before.
My new companion pats her prayer mat with a crazy grin.

LEARNING FROM OTHERS

An early winter cloudless
coup de feuilles
comes between the thin end of a twig
and the grip of a stubborn leaf.
Frost contracts all the tree's floret
and builds a bridge from veteran
bark to this year's brittle stem
until it melts. Links experience
thaw return to water. A thousand
extreme youngsters cut away –
unsupported small leaves,
big leaves, without effort – die.
Calling unlatched dozens
a byte of wind twists, tricks
and loosens invertebrate, chiropractic
knots. Clicks tighten, disconnect and glide
from all that misfit cargo
clung to, carried and untied.

WITNESS

When late figs were as tight as cold nipples
and what made them fall was sharp frost
not the ripe weight of their lute-shaped globes,
a sparrowhawk came to roost on the television
aerial of The Ridgeway hospice where I now lived.

The hawk was waiting for breakfast to bob
its watery neck just one beat slower
than the usual stream of intermittent quavers.

Where the roof had been extended flat
and the courtyard fig tree wrought a grey
iron helix in the garden below, pigeons
sometimes brought their urban bread.

The sparrowhawk, as sudden
as a fall of rock, clamped its toes
on the back and thigh of one fat bird.
Tight, rapt wings stretched and closed
on a view of life utterly engulfed.

The pigeon's eyes cast about like faces sinking
at sea knowing that a lifeboat wouldn't come.

The hawk adjusted its grip and feathered the breast
exactly at the soft rib spot above the pigeon's heart.

Thudding heavily, meat slammed on a butcher's block,
the finished game saw its flesh hatch open, a string
of skin and vein drape a vine across its head,
purple blood steaming in the winter air.

BRICKS AND PORCELAIN

Two cities on two islands;
one makes bricks,
the other, porcelain –
bricks for houses,
porcelain for feasts.

They trade, until a murder
at the annual games; two porcelain
drunks attack one sober brickie.
Then war – bricks against porcelain,
no contest.

Following blood,
savagery and plunder – the homeless
children of potters
bury their fathers, lament
their wasted mothers,

reshape their delicate skills,
drag themselves like crabs
across the dust, a talent for tunnelling
and bombs, serving green sweet wine
to burly, thirsty masters.

REJECTED STONES

If I want to make it out of here
I'll have to build a road
from bricks my soul rejected.

How do I set one stepping
stone in front of nothing,
when I can't even smell
the kiln I'm baking in?

If I look into the bright
I'm bad at I might find a map,
and if the frightened dark

of what I'm good at opens up,
I might find a route towards
the stink that fuels me forward.

WHY READ POETRY?

Why not read a poem
just for what it says
in language without the consolation
of meaning?

It might knit
random anything. Is there
a technical achievement
more disruptive than a poem?

Builders who accidentally betray
a lie at any point, display
the hollow shape they make
by what degraded bricks they lay,

whether the grand aisle
of maudlin insight, or
culpabilities lodged
in narrative expression.

A metic pun
at the expense of civic logic
confirms all that paving stones
assault by honest rioting.

Surreal voices boo the line
when an image is confined
to one inevitable fit
and not to paradox

fast lane, slow line, poetry outwits.

REPLY

I know why I read poetry
when I'm listening to others try
like me, but fail to say what they mean.

It's not when there's a book in my hand,
a poem on screen or recited aloud
that I know why I read poetry.

It's when my comrades try to barb the best
cleanly, incisively, idiosyncratically, earnestly
trying, like me, but we fail to say what we mean.

It gives me a bite into the gristle of words,
through their fat, slippery disguise –
that's when I know why I read poetry.

I probe hackneyed speech
for the seam, ore, nugget of those who
search, like me, but fail to say what we mean.

Every day the same life stories
suffered, endured, clung to, over and over again,
but we fail to say what we mean.
That's when I know why I read poetry.

IN RECOVERY

Twice a week since being here
I've listened to my comrades struggle,
and I among them,
sharing details of the trouble
we're all in, how we can't get clear.
Life's become a puzzle.

Some of us dress up our fear,
parading it confirms we more
or less adore our struggle,
almost glad it isn't clear.
Sharing details of our puzzle
is what keeps us here.

Not everyone unveils their puzzle,
some conceal why they are here.
I often think of Jacob and his struggle,
how the Angel provoked resolve.
I've been advised that real trouble
is when we've thrown the problem clear.

Others argue life itself is trouble
because we embody pain and fear,
suffering's an endless puzzle
we could learn to love.   But,
the more an old wound festers
it breeds a putrid atmosphere.

When I panic in a struggle
it takes longer to get clear.
I'm not in love with trouble,
I've learned that much from being here.
Who wants a puzzle
whose solution spells more fear?

I'd rather have authentic trouble
and contend with what I fear
engaged with more than spooks
that prompt retreat.
At least I want a bigger struggle
my greed for that is clear.

Adopted fear mimics foster trouble,
corpses rot, phantoms decompose – it's clear
I have to kill the worm that rules this puzzle,
and prune the root of a withered rose.

GET A LIFE

Here's a pub quiz question
you're never going to get. Ready?
Who coined the expression,
"Get a life"? John Lennon? Gore Vidal? Umberto Eco?
No – it was Soren Kierkegaard.
And what he meant was sober up – not from beer or gin
but from the intoxicating trance of art.
If you're getting drunk just stop it.
Kierkegaard was a master who let his dog
drink from every muddy pool they passed
but then at every tree he yanked the lead
and wouldn't let his poodle splash.
His thirsty friend had made a choice based on filthy appetite
whereas K drank merely to experience the stages on life's way.
A real fool keeps walking until the middle of the forest,
where the witch's gruesome hut is spinning –
wakeful dizziness at the heart of life
not a steadying twirl from one emergency lamp post to the next.

A WOLF FOLLOWS A MAN

A wolf follows a man into the refuge
of St Mary's Church, Beenham, Berkshire.

Imagining weapons the man prays,
also nervous, the wolf explores the church.

The man cannot transcend the wolf,
the wolf is not interested in the man.

The man can only think of the wolf,
only of the wolf, the wolf, the wolf.

How did we end up in church together?
In bed together?   In life together? The man
prays harder, imagining more weapons.

The wolf, when he comes upon the man,
will pit his current terror and bewilderment
against the man's rueful, lifelong resignation.

RAINSTICKS

(in memoriam Peter John Hay, 1951 - 2003)

'Charms against jackals' is a phrase
Pete Hay said at Kennet Bank.
This poem is a form of thanks
to the founder of Two Rivers Press.

Rainsticks. How do they do it?
There are many speculations.

Some say they are filled with blue plastic pencil sharpeners
that crack the first time you use them.
That brittle clatter is the ripple of keyboards hacking
the sharpeners' unique mimetic vortex,
for as long as fingers pat the alphabet
sharpeners snare into a contorted phalanx
cracking knuckles as they all look for a penknife.

Others say they are filled with frozen lama droppings
thawing and refreezing three times a second,
and on every kaleidoscopic pellet a lightning flash
illuminated king searching for an ebony queen.
That noise is the sound of his steel boot caps
marching over expanding crystal spectrums
so old, smoky fissures are umbilical galactic plasma,
teratomic plumes, trailing back to what came first
big bang, big fluctuation, scraper, arrowhead and axe.

I believe they are filled with the exploded diagrams of bottle
dynamos whose slate origami djinns whirl gragger rattles, kites
snagging overhead cables above a rapid-fire shooting range; acoustic
holograms of stone incandescent light-bulbs; campaign buckle
adjustments of Shambhala engineering mechanics; asterisk footnote

scree pattering the iron exterior of a bulging orgone chamber;
my mother's bones in an imposter's urn;
printers' upset composing trays;
the gaudy cups and saucers of Patagonian colonists
                                        chattering happily
on the opening day of their first freshwater canal.

                                        And so
their aural decoy is a whirlwind of percussive ploys, charms
against jackals, the hard thorn of a ripe idea lodging awkwardly
in the tiled spiral eardrums of porcelain cyber subjects
who think that life's a social QWERTY board but not a beach –
preferring virtual control, instead of shift, tilt, echo, silence
                                        and repeat.

NEW DIET FLATULENCE

Green beans love ruby beetroot love,
but most beans ballad broadsheets
while beets prefer a room keep quiet
without the happy riot of curly greens
revealing where they all have been.

Stained patty scarlet, boa edged
cherry, my recently flatulent colon
enjoys a private bulkhead party
with pickled beets and fennel,
blushing ginger on sabbatical.

Don't quickly call a gut quack shrink
it's only the WC trimming up in pink
and carmine red to celebrate
the beetroot crimson, Venetian fox
trot number two evacuation rate.

Molasses drop slow but beans
fray rough because the global
atmosphere changes, downwind
prompts raw uproar, indignation.
Even the cat doesn't want to know.

Which makes me an odor (aura liar) drifting
doldrums of the kitchen to mint a fart
silently and sheepishly, Forties, Cromarty.
In order to disguise this sailor's art
I bruise the wind a nose can't localize.

Allies in this salubrious, vegan sanctuary?
Peanut butter, pomegranate, aniseed and parsley.
While bean dreamers lazer for the stars
meditative beets mediate my alimentary tract.
We ruminate so far apart, legumes don't react.

FIREWORMS AND SULPHUR

When battery hens need sulphur
they eat their own molted feathers.

With a runny nose from misplaced fasting,
at night I prowl the ancient building
grazing for chalk, ash, coal, orange peel,
pencil nibs, bits of window frame.

An impish fireworm glowing
in the fever of my gullet thinks
all thoughts are meat, all hopes
ferment to worry as a special treat.

It will constellate eventually from an image
to an ulcer – then I'll burn for what it wants,

breaking into an always open cage –
mania's covenant, night walker's rage.

TROUBLE IN VALHALLA

If Arawn *had* been cuckolded by Pwyll
the world might have gone
to red-eared dogs cocking their legs
against the tree in Eden – clerics chasing
whisky with toxic aftershave, pure
land last rites calling late night
taxis on a stolen mobile phone.
What a mess. There's trouble in Valhalla
when the dead stop feasting and fast.
Don't take it literally – don't start a war.
Don't throw a winning game
or dismount just as you're finally
cycling free of birth and death.
But, there's nothing stopping you
telling your neighbour, hey man
your van is filling my tent with fumes.
Asia, your greedy cities are melting
the glacier that cools my hotel drink.
Lady, that's the second time
your overweight, asthmatic Pekinese
has puked on my picnic. Europe,
Gore-Tex tourists are wearing
down the paths that crowd
our simian mountaintop.
The gods don't want to merge – conflict
is their paradise. The absolute
commander may never tire of heretic blood
but you don't have to sleep on the axe
that's chopping the world tree down.

LETTUCE PEARL

Following an overnight fast, I feel good
despite battling a mild but constant headache.
I'm trying my best to keep the night
for sleep. It's morning and I'm still awake.

I sit up, stretch, yawn, lean over the side
of my narrow bed and cough. My dribble
looks like potter's slip, tastes like talcum powder
thick with the sweat of a watchdog's tongue.

Hair like seaweed. My left thumbnail
has a smudge the size of a half lentil
stamped with a smiley face on it, rising
from the lanula through the corrugated plate.

I'm paying attention to changes in my body
as a way of keeping the horizon straight,
while all my instruments show that
the world is flying upside down.

My maverick fate might just be
to find the pearl hidden in a lettuce
all these vegetarians rabbit on about.
We eat an awful lot of salad here.

Following weeks without any, a memory
of sleep returns. An egg struck
by lightning, carried by disembodied hands.
I wait until a thousand hands appear.

The pearl hatches. A sticky firebird
flops out and hauls its sparkling abdomen
from a narrow strip of silver gutter
towards a garden wriggling with bean sprouts.

CORVINE DATE – TRUE STORY

Dark and early, wet, before dawn,
in the first week of November,
at the hospice where I'd come to stay,
I was standing, quietly, near the trees
when a crow landed beside me
like a black scarf falling
from my shoulder to the lawn.
At first I thought the crow
couldn't have known I was there
but when it hopped around me and pecked
at the dark, shiny tips of my untied bootlace
I realised it was. For a moment I thought
it might be the same bird that flew
from the glove of Mabon son of Modron
into the mouth of a shepherd
known to Henry Vaughan.
It had appeared as effortlessly as
a piece of clothing I never knew I had
until I bent to pick it up.
I took off all my clothes
and made a circle of leaves
where the crow and I could consider
the nature of our meeting. It
didn't fly away. Not knowing what to do
I offered a gift. Crow hopped towards
the soggy, dark green pendulum of my dandelion tea bag.
We stayed together for about an hour, studying
each other closely as we moved and waited.
When I felt cold, seeing it respond to what I said,
I dressed and ran into the kitchen bringing
broken biscuits and a rope of onion stems.

The bird waited and I marvelled
at its sheer black on black, so black
that the blue burn at the end of its wings
confirmed the slow fact of our encounter.
Its tough whiskers, spurred toes, the white strobe
of its eyes and contented watery gurgling
were all a miracle, especially this close to the waking world.
If I had vanished into pious awe,
if I had given up my own critical faculty,
I might have entered the murder of crows
from which this shock emerged.
That didn't happen. I wasn't lost.
Why Crow had come, I couldn't explain
but it didn't go away and it did change everything
about that retreat I'd planned, considered
and thought I'd carefully arranged.

"*MYN BRAIN I – FE WNES*"

Eighth week of my intended
four month withdrawal
from the outside world
to a new and difficult place,
involving inner reflection
and unfamiliar physical work,
a companion also called
– a carrion crow –
and it didn't fly away.

The RSPB and RSPCA
both advised –
scare that probably
once befriended,
unwisely humanized
creature off or you'll
contribute to its early death.

Myn llw, myn brain i, fe wnes
â nerth fy mhen, â'm holl dyfais.

But it wouldn't go. I tried
to be as fierce as a vixen
driving off her cubs.

Defied, the crow would glide into the trees
but return within an hour.
Soon it started waiting near my window.

Magpies dive-bombed
the lawn where we first met,
jackdaws haunt the drive,
jays linger just beyond the garden
where I worked – Crow
never far away at shoulder height.

Some mornings an angry parliament
of rooks would assemble, high up,
nearby and bark malignant taunts
before quick strike muscle power fired
beaks, claws and wings into the courtyard
to featherbeat the walls
in vicious, noisy, tag teams
hissing and mewing
for my friend's ominous blood.

One night, with the hostel
all asleep, I waited mesmerised
beneath the fig tree where
Brân the Blessed often perched,
both as Bendigeidfran
and as Branwen
son and daughter
of their liquid father Llŷr,
whose half-speech I now learned.

While soft, slow, pearls of rain
sparkling by kitchen light
fell in glistening strings,
dollops of scintillating guano
puddled freshly opened oysters
on the courtyard's medieval tiles.

UKULELE

Practicing ukulele in the walled garden –
I sound so good!   Haven't quite gone flea
leaping with Hawaiian beach boys yet
but with no one else around it's like singing
in a tiled bathroom. I love my clumsy music.

If the garden is a refuge, stealing biscuits,
smoking in the greenhouse on rainy days
is not a devious luxury. Life is less confirmed
than condemned numbing work with
hands loaded not relieved carrying less.

When silver moon runs from golden sun
nothing can force a ukulele strum
or a yodel from my lips, I'm willing to swallow
a thistle and end it all, falling asleep
on a pillow of soiled hay in the chicken run.

My brain's been buying stuff
it doesn't want while all I used to value
runs away. The coins I flip spin
only debt and I an addicted gambler
leaping at whatever happens next.

Well adrift, all the anchors I throw out
melt like snowflakes. If I carry
on like this my soul will be repossessed
but not before I lose my home and family.
"Ukulele! Ukulele! Set my magic tortoise free!"

MACARONIC COMMENTS ON A CROW

Gwyn y gwêl y frân ei chyw,
is this what we are going through,
creaduriaid alltud 'n rygnu byw?

Enfys liwgar, enfys glais
and now this creature in my life,
nid rhith yw hi, mae'n bod, mae'n ffaith.

Ger Tafwys crwydraf heb fawr synied,
this animal presence is unexpected,
rhaid bod rhywle camgymeried.

Ac nawr yn ffrind mae gen i frân,
I'm getting used to it as best I can,
fe ddaw'n llai estron yn y man.

Rwy'n gwrthod cynnig cig a bara,
three weeks or more we've been together,
ym mhle terfyna'r syndod yma?

Wi ddim yn credu mewn byd arall
nor miracles and messengers,
ond dyma wyrth wi ddim yn deall.

'All neb yma tynnu ynghyd
this crow's a fact and not a dream,
fe ddaeth o'r coed yn glwtyn rhydd.

BENDIGELDFRAN

A carrion crow walks along pale cables of a tulip tree
trained over two sides of the small retreat courtyard
where brittle, honey coloured leaves scratch against
stone window mullions split like worn hessian ropes –

                      – the same crow that dropped,
unexplained, one morning, to the grass beside me,
a black scarf from the shoulder of an unknown messenger
and now, as on recent mornings, performing tricks
like a rolling finch in the birdcage of a hermit.

Smooth branches, the same thin green as country cider,
stubbed with shut buds the size of a terrier's canine teeth,
speckled with ochre sprays of broken privet tips
shredded over two days of November storms, receive
his antics like the slow words of a writer's brush.

Aware that I was anchoring this scene in the all but
monochromatic Chinese solitary bird tradition,
as well as naming my animal guest after Brân,
whose pickled head indulged the Birds of Rhiannon,
I felt the picture didn't need any other superstitions.

But when, having tentatively shared my totem news,
I heard that Crow could also be the wrathful mask of dazzling,
eleven headed, thousand handed, Avolokitesvara,
I wasn't quite as happy about this visitor getting close to me.

THE STORY OF A BATH

The homeopath advised baths of Epsom salts.
I understood that salts calm and might even silence
whatever it is that agitates a painful mind.
Did the room grow quieter as the water turned blue?
Already trying everything I was ready to try anything.

I'd been given a small, dark green, brick of soap
wrapped in hand-made paper,
tied with thin, red, cellophane ribbon,
the knot sealed with wax.   Tea tree soap –
as perfumed as creosote, another intense ingot of hope.

I moved around the bathroom
like a butoh dancer slowing down the world,
reaching for my towel, toothbrush and razor,
as though they were sacramental objects
assisting at the baptism of reformed bruises.

Sitting on the edge – the clear, coloured water
without a blemish either of suds or of dirt, the bath
old, etiolated – enamel chafed in unexpected places,
iron showing through. Briefly I regarded myself
as a font. What I stepped into reflected me.

Thinking about the woman who'd given me the soap
I unshouldered the ribbon and opened it –
                                        setting the tissue paper
on top of my carefully folded clothes. Suddenly the soap
twisted from my hands and leapt into the toilet bowl
where, a few weeks earlier, I'd found the wedding ring.

I fished out the soap and used it to wash my hair.
This was one more conundrum in a procession
of puzzles I seemed to be at the centre of;
the crow that flies around me, bothering the staff,
and now this literal toilet bowl serving as my Siloam.

FABULOUS PARADIGM SHIFT

I realised I couldn't change the world
on my own, so I looked around for help.
The village didn't offer much and the next parish
wasn't any better than the worst we had at home.

At a crossroads where two scarecrows stood –
one telling the truth, the other only lies
I managed to get my opportunity
and, unlike my brothers, got the question right.

This hurled me into a world of recently
qualified, therapist shamanettes
earnestly trying the latest practices on us –
I, their common denominator at Guinea Pig Zero.

Thrumming to Tibetan bowls growling on my belly,
Bowen technique realigning the way I walk,
herd of cows spinning rhythms in the dance hall,
I ate from every furrow these ploughs churned up.

Noticing the start was an unexpected shock.   One
day I didn't care what anyone thought of the crow
that came to find me every day. This circumstantial crow,
an uncomfortable fact creating havoc in the refuge.

I grew to like my own deformities and return
to what might come to be.   This animal guide
was not imaginary. I didn't have to kill it.   It caused
so much trouble, uneasy sorcerers discussed evicting me.

STORY TELLER

A story teller came by, his voice
like any one of us, but also unlike
anything I'd ever heard,
hands beating goat skin,
galloping drumbeats
letting the unexpected in.

In a world of impossible tasks
when the idiot hero managed
to do what the bad king asked,
the fairy story had a chorus
with a talking horse, "Don't worry
the worst is yet to come".

The hero always disobeyed
the caution of his horse's voice
and for every prize he gained
pain increased, until at last
he had no choice but plunge
into hideously, boiling water.

We listened like grizzled babes
and cheered when the bad king died,
many of us confessed
how chronically we'd abandoned
ever calling on our horse,
some hung their heads and cried.

The story teller listened
and encouraged us to sing.
Now stand up on your feet
he called, and sing again.

I'd love to have a job like that,
patting my hands against granite.

THE INVISIBLE TAOIST SWORDSMAN

The invisible Taoist
swordsman
cursive with a blade,
had the kick
of a bull dragon,
sent me hurtling
backwards
into the Tree of Life
cracking my spine
like a hollow, elder stalk.

I didn't like that,
muttered to myself,
It shouldn't be like this
all rotten and broken
while his martial dance,
is as fluid
as flames of silk
rising in a cirrus storm
of saffron particles
to meet me.

I knew
I couldn't defeat him
so I had to win him over
as the vanquished
persuade a king
by performing well, instead
of confirming
overwhelming power
as an enemy.

I
removed my spine
and set it on the ground
as though it were a sheep's
after being ravaged
by a pack of dogs.

Now,
as free as burning
dragon mucus floating
through the air,
it was up to me
where I landed.
At the gate,
in the ditch,
on my backbone?

I pulled myself together.

SLIDING DOWN GLASS MOUNTAIN

Sliding down glass mountain. Look! No hands!
Wasn't as smooth as it looked. Flaws were random,
there was no telling where cactus grew
or where cracks scarred my fall to ground level.

Unimaginable wealth had been briefly mine,
every riddle solved by asking. Heavenly!
The files I stole shredded as I fell but
cushioned my arrival when I landed.

Facing new trouble, the magic saddle that carried me
soon ran out of whatever fuel made it work
and instead of being helpful, the benevolent
horse started making jokes at my expense.

When I asked, Equus said, "Excuse me, do we share a script?
  "According to mine, you don't have anything else to say."

CARNIVAL

In the morning when I push
back all the masks that leered
out at me last night, stiffening
to fix the strange, they fall away
and ordinary objects – indifferent
but conscientious janitors of dreams –
tidy up the party room and without
comment fix the broken, mop the spilled,
tidy the dishevelled, shush the snivelling,
listen to the bruised. I have a choice,
attack my teacups, resent my books,
loathe my garden or be as good to them.
None of this is fair to a house that
had done nothing wrong, either last
night, last year or slowly as its objects gathered to me,
each one determined, alone, promising some
offer of itself while I seemed steady
at the heart of what I thought
a house might be. At night, that same deal
unfolds, magnifying terms I hoped would
be forgotten, a debt I'd never have to meet,
a pledge I'd never have to honour; repeating
a fold from now back to the thin sentimental
pulse that already knew its brittle future.

I BUST OLD FURNITURE

I bust old furniture
by putting it in positions
never intended
                straightback chairs
    rock   break
      in this lively
golden firelight
        how beautiful
    they must have been
        the memory of a chair
is like the memory of sex
    a smoke
medicine
        or a restaurant
    remembering
doesn't mean
you re-experience it
            unlike trauma
        where in the rupture
of amnesia and memory
        experience
            comes on strong
                chairs
            in flames flames
    are what the seats
let occupy them
                    now
        flames
    are restless visitors
as relentless as my need
to abandon places

I once defended
    the furniture's advice
     try this
      go
 wild
  be flexible
 as fire itself   burn
consume every sign
I've ever read
     live on
   the fuel
 me now
   me then
 I do it.

FLETCHER

Eating an all day breakfast near Culham
we discuss the virtues of uranium.

Quicksilver adhesive snuffs fireflies
on the thin rubbery envelope of reed-bed

ditches where filters clot. Radioactive gum
spindles embryos of beryllium.

Ladled from mercury in college halls
biometric lazers stripe protective overalls.

Here air is meshed for high security estates,
each fibre optic finds you where you meditate.

Frogs and newts avoid your very buttonholes
feathered with quarks' prismatic arrows.

Nuclear emulsion leaches fallow land.
Homeopathic globules thin, dilute, deliver, and

– tincture of Big Bang's recreated spark –
glow worm's candle fades, decaying in the dark.

RIVER OCK

Asphyxiated minnows float and stiffen
in the slow drift of a weirpool on the River Ock.
Each fish sketches its own decomposition.

The five senses pack a weekend suitcase,
check their tickets
and drive away towards *Bron Ebargofiant.*

Two small children recall quite differently
being hungry in the same house at the same time,
even though they aren't children anymore.

I know that Ock is the Welsh word *Eog,*
Eogwy, Ogwr, the river where I usually live.
Now I stare at Mercia through Wessex fog.

Minnows decay following a rapid autopsy,
prodded by a miasmic British phantom.
An unexpected tantrum kills its passive twin.

CLEANING A ROOM

Raking leaves, chopping wood, feeding chickens, filling a skip, are easy but being asked to clean a silent, empty room that is manifestly spotless is difficult. I feel unsure and reluctant at being put on indoor duty. But, as I clean the hospice meeting room I find the remnant of a spider's thread, a fly, a human hair, a fallen petal and concede that the room did need attention after all. Even succinct, well-toned, essentially oiled, veterans of the pumice stone lose a few skin cells every day and there must have been invisible billions in that solemn, effulgent room – a subtle, spectral epidermis bathing in October sunbeams. When the mop, duster, polish, bucket and vacuum cleaner had been returned to their closet cells I went to the garden. Everything was wet and I took my time. Later I set a bowl of fresh cut flowers on the white, glass-topped, wicker table. Finally, as advised, I clapped my hands and snapped my fingers in a magic charm, breaking the wake of recently departed guests, making the space, as well as objects in it, clean and primed, ready for the troubled, ready for the weary and ready for convivial visitors.

PLEA

Harsh limits of wood and stone,
metal, skin, vegetable mesh,
protect me from nothing.

Infinity – empty, irresistible.

A house singing to the sky,
field uncorked by stars,
heart inhumanly alive –
without fatigue,
each whim as determined
as a cloud.

Minioga'm gweud on my grandmother's tongue,
fix my decision on pain,
torment on a broken promise.

Detach my smile from daydreams,
attach it to the gleam
in her entirely distant eyes.

SEVERN FANTASY

I sometimes wish
instead of being a river god
capable of reversing direction,
I might be something a lot less –
perhaps a sofa in a 1970s billiards hall,
or since I'm water borne
possibly a rubber dinghy
bought exclusively from money
shoved through the slot
of a snug RNLI charity box.

Or even –
when I really change,
why not a sugar fortified cocktail cherry
floating in a tall, stemmed glass
slopping a complex drink named
after a translucent smut avatar I devised?
I'll have a Crystal Channel please.

If I were that cherry,
a mealy nose on the face
of an absinthe green and blue harlequin
buoyant in water-wings, floating
through a current of soda and sweet wine,
barnacled with bubbles,
I'd gaze up at the moon
and one for each finger
I'd count the aeons prone to wars
that used to irritate my soul.

Almost motionless, rocking
just a little before the flake
returning from a date sighs
and knocks me back; there,
loaded on my single stilt, I'd savour
my immediate shift from immensity
to being forgotten and neglected,
set aside on a fussy windowsill.

I'd spend eternity listening
to the echo of pink daydream sound FX
in a room that never changes, held
like a brief mistake before rejected
from the gawping pout
of a pale doppelganger reflecting momentarily
how to keep the entire universe
menacingly lit, sexually graphic,
profitable, cheap and nice.

HANDLING AN OBJECT

What happens to an object used for torture, and the same
object, when innocent, draws no attention to itself?

St Catherine, twisted by tongs, eased her killers into yells of fun,
her squeezed prayers and nipples shaping what they did –

technique wrought her their broken object.   What condemned
her compliant flesh to be their clueless gore?   Tongs?

A piece of the True Cross found its way to Santo Toribio, Spain.
What of the nails? Were they pulled out and used again?

Used to touch second nails? All factory nails
elevated to the Holy Grail?

Splinters taken from their reliquaries stretch as far as where
credulity cargos the inanimate, bribing what we venerate.

For the parched, the plastic cup of a thermos flask contains
more value than an ivory box with more than dubious remains.

Forsaken objects disclose suspicions
things are based not on fact but on conviction.

Tongs that held the coals that burned St Catherine's hair
are now the tongs these monsters use to nurse their fire.

Convert the darkness where these tortures lurk,
and celebrate the object of her finish as a firework.

I use knives, tongs, buckets, ropes, jacks, chainsaws
sometimes noticing how well or ill they fit my hand,
rarely remembering the killing fields they aim for.

Twisted enough, distorted by execrable mechanics
even the humblest, most passive treasure of a room
can lure intent towards chiromantic conflict.

Effulgent patina of a cherished object
builds a subtle navy against
ranks of disrespect time
anticipates can form against it.

Catalogued by the story that found it,
skills orbit the trajectory
that launches any thing
ready to outshine itself.

Harsh comments, rough treatment,
neglect – rust, cobweb, lacklustre
eyes after taking insults from an oaf,
all of these can be withstood.

A million qualities and their prayer
sing when cleaned already glowing,
framed already singled out, set apart,
treasured when secure, at peace, at home.

Shrine of the thing, its vital place
bristling with vigour, attention,
choice – exceeding all of these
in contact with the human hand.

Material that a conscious touch
has considerately charmed, crackles,
glows, kindled by the chorus
launched at birth to praise it.

Every rudder needs a soul to steer it.

THE EYE OF
THE GREAT WHITE HORSE

I receive a cart of dunge
from stables near Uffington,
my furnace burns too hot with coal
a quieter flame will achieve my goal.

There is a mystery to my supplier
who keeps his farm below the Manger
of Great White Horse near Dragon Hill,
this fuel is brought with cryptic skill.

I've seen the stalls stand clean and empty
yet dunge they yield in steaming plenty.
'Tis said the Great Horse roams the area
and bestows on some this special favour.

And so I know my work is blessed
by mystic dunge so well compressed
by this *hengist* in the sky
who gazes down with his chalk Eye.

Last midsummer in a shower of rain
I climbed The Ridgeway once again,
I stood within that Eye and wished
my urgent labours be accomplished.

And so it is not accidently
that one local farmer prudently
supplies me from his stable
with devotions that are invisible.

All know that prayers made in the Eye
come true for those who earnestly
forge their vision to a single task –
The Great Horse gives to those who ask.

DAY TRIP

Being in time everything slows
to 186,000 miles per second
including our escape to Swanage for the day,
barely a terra byte from Oxford,
relaxing from the rigours of being in retreat
or on retreat, as your job description calls it. So much depends
not only on wheelbarrows and biodynamic gardening
but the difference in shape and meme
between lower case 'o' and 'i'.
'If' or 'of' each phonemic moment?
The shredded jolt of sudden insight
or souvenir shrapnel from tenebrous therapy?
Both hurt, as we noticed, getting nowhere
further than one hundred miles by car.
Why did you bring me here I thought,
until the atmospheric violence of a Purbeck sunset
calmed to mutual pink your textual ink united
with the nib of mine. It happened on Studland
Chalk, inscribing us into the soggy hill.

FALSE CHANTERELLES

Stems of the mushrooms we picked went deeper
than we first thought when, reaching into coarse grass,
we found other treasures.   Intense chanterelles.
Their tightly gleaming button heads not yet unfolded
into inside out umbrellas. In a high field, shafts of sunlight,
                                                  acres wide,
we picked unusual mushrooms, orange-brown, pale saffron flags
just nibbled at their prime, all tumbled to the bag, also long thin
psilocybes, threaded like pale worms in pleated water patterns,
scarfed tongues ruffling their spore up the solid mountain side.
But you wandered off and threw almost every fungus in the field
into your basket – false chanterelles, wax caps, destroying angels,
as though my cautions were a foolish superstition to be ignored.
What you picked was daring and enchanting but it wasn't food.

WINTER ACONITE

"aconite sprung where hell's hound dribbled"
British Simples, 'Sir' John Fernie

What survives is tough
and won't be mistreated.

Pounded with hymns
softened by tears, parts
of what I am will never be edible again.

I have a seam of yellow aconite
slipping a collective fuse
through mud, twigs and snow –
by May a blissful wreck of ruined pods.

Atoms lift into a diamond body
a thousand statisticians couldn't count.

Corruptions
where these titanium gleams dismantle lightning
reveal unnoticed paths
towards distant Crystal Mountain.

Black seeds hatch from bird borne waste
breaking the unattainable summit into illogical steps
that only intuitive evidence confirms,
a life that queen bees rouse
as they guard dormant love
from storms set to kill a soul.

A monstrous jaw following its snout
fostered this deadly appeal.

Trickster's child, disobedient to the last,
eat the golden hand I offer – reaching from the past.

OXFORD WELSH

A long way from Maesteg
miners' children shivering in the rain,
close to Nuffield's botched
attempt to ban us all from Cowley.

The choir sings at Uffington,
Woodstock, wins Swindon Eisteddfod,
but then Gresford Colliery disaster fund –
two hundred and sixty six men dead.

I'm not in the choir, no one
from the Dafydd ap Gwilym Society
knows I'm here, in the shadow
of Alfred's Saxon Road to Avebury.

St Swithun pray for me, restore my
broken eggs, translate my bones
into a pilgrim's pack waking to walk
the drovers' road to Wales.

When Rhondda marched and Risca begged,
militant walkouts won for all the workers
when Cotswold shepherds dare not raise
their docile, brass band heads.

Far from the sawn-down, shortened desk I use,
sitting on a *zafu* carried from Japan;
far from devotions that once fed the fix
I had on a hopeless desire to belong,

I find myself sharing a bench
at a long communal table
eating macrobiotic food,
befriended by a crow I can't explain.

I live in a flat county
with Wittenham Clumps to climb.
Oty tila Mynydd Cynffig wedi f'angofio?
near Thames, I think this everyday.

Wi heb ddiarddel bro fy mebyd,
Siloam, Cefn Cribbwr lle cwata 'nghân,
y pridd lle crwydrais rhwng sawl afon,
Nant Iorwerth Goch a'r nentydd mân.

Here I stand in the walled garden
until the west wind cuts my eyes,
at breakfast's morning share I explain –
I'm ready to live at home again.

WALKING THE PLANK

Without a hard hat, knee pads,
safety goggles, luminous vest,
none of which I had, nor a banksman
to watch the road as I turned my life around,

I grabbed at one last, fragile straw
based on little more than magic workshops.

Lips so perfect, kisses
shot through their target
instead of hitting flesh.

There were traps
the most insured traveller
would never have expected – a pious
bedroom and, on the landing, random
floorboards swung up in my face.

The first of many. I mistook
each footstep for a foothold.

The tower bed an arcane map
lost in perfumed knots. I slept
among exotic practices and now
who to blame for this garden rake
smacking the compass I steer by?

As captain of the nose I was born with
instead of fixing my cuts
I clung to bilge; even when the food
screamed poison, I kept cooking it.

My star, my flame, oasis, breeze, lagoon,
didn't conspire to cage me in a flooded maze
on a circular raft with a treacherous deck, but
every timber burned, drifting from island to island
as if each refuge confirmed the drain we couldn't avoid.

I kept worshipping the labyrinth
and the broken match that lit my way,
finally my only nourishment was blood,
when I lost enough of that
I noticed I was dying.

REBIRTH BY WINDOW

I fled the hospice at midnight
passing my things through the moonlit window.
It isn't what I thought would happen but when
the director danced Mary Magdalene for me
and Circe for the others I had to recognise
that I simply didn't want to. I'd drawn
that joker too many times before. As remote
as it was, what I loved was suddenly confirmed
as something else. I also knew that climbing
through a window to try and get closer to it
was to start my travels via an exit sometimes reserved for death.

To escape can be as dangerous as being taken prisoner.

It wasn't sexual cobweb, kidnap, trophy or cocoon
that disturbed me – I had been warned.
But I was concerned about my sudden freedom,
noticing that once again I was in the open air
without a wall of any kind to protect, shape or restrain me.

The narrow window and its symbolism
was my decision, my choice too would be whether
to confide my dreams to a cocktail of self-recrimination
or look up at the fractal play of trees and stars
and promise myself an ecumenical return
to good books, familiar food, chapel worship I grew up on
and the company of friends – their poems, gardens,
experiments, stories, travels and guitars.

                        The failed seduction
was in fact a mauetic push through a window frame
from an emergency confinement
I'd outgrown.

KEY

By lifting down the key that I can't get,
what nights enlarge, days unfold,
when I unlock doors I haven't thought of yet?

Wilder scenes than I have ever met
welcome me in nightmares and in dreams,
by lifting down the key.

Do I want the key? I'm all set
to learn from this chaotic mess
and fall through doors I've never opened.

It's confusing here, sweet is sour,
and nothing will return or stay the same
by lifting down the key.

I've put a lot into this pilgrimage,
I anticipate more failure and upset
when I pass through doors I haven't opened yet.

This retreat has been a hospital and safety net,
I've tested every floorboard, every friend.
Reaching for the key,
I step through doors I haven't opened yet.

SURFING THE SEVERN BORE

Waiting for the Severn Bore
on an upturned kitchen table,
thinking of other table tops –
Nizwa, Buckhead, Togoshi Koen.

As I lean towards the khaki water
a liquid hand reaches up
and grabs my school teacher's tie,
pulling me towards my face,
"Smile," it said, "while you still can,
"because soon you'll be wearing the frown you had
"before the day that you were born."

I knew the phantom well.
"I thought I'd lost everything," I said,
  certainly I thought I'd never see you again."

"Well I'm back," the abrupt reflection said,
 " but things will never be the same between us.
    You were supposed to look after me back there.
    I thought I'd lost you in that accident."

"Which accident?"

"Sneaking through the window,
  sliding down Crystal Mountain,
  eating all that pica crap,
  falling out of bed,
  you name it."

A striped green, tartan dog with chess
board ears climbed out of the water
and wobbled the flooded table even more
when it shook itself off in a squat of rays.

The dog sniffed and marked each table leg in turn
and I no longer felt the raft was mine.
I didn't look forward to sharing meals and
as the dog stared at me I knew
it wanted to divide our floating territory.

The chequered hound leaned to drink
from that portion of the table
where earlier I'd seen my puzzled face.
I took my chance, and from its flabby haunches
shoved it quickly overboard.

Wet, lying on my belly, I held it firmly underwater
until its cramped spasms stopped bolting
and the struggle ended.

Again I had the table to myself.

I stood and delicately touched my face,
still there, rippled by disasters,
corrugated, podgy, like a scrubbed
scaffolding plank stranded on a sandbank,
but still my own and still intact.

I heard the wind thicken through
the stubbly fields. Within seconds the bore
flooded up and the river changed direction.

I surfed towards Stonebridge,
sharing the surge with a thousand
bloated corpses.

HOLY ASH

1
Even starting from a long way out
after Nakhodkar, Soji-ji wasn't far away,
and from chaos near Abingdon the well-hung
pomegranates of Jabal Ahkdar changed
into a chew of ruby pips to briefly
satisfy my greed for more.

2
Acorns of Hafod Heulog dropping
at random in October storms intend
to flower into bog oak. Looking
down from Cefn at the hole
we see the Cribbwr seam exposed,
Hafod Heulog trapped to be destroyed.

3
The River Kenfig like Nant Iorwerth Goch
reduced to a fishless ditch
while we stay warm listening to CDs.
Some things I look forward to
reflect their carbon gift then turn to ash
as I walk closer to them.

4
Ash has no nervous system
but when I'm in the woods the trees
see straight through me. Leaping gleams
in the doomed surface of the stream
coagulate a silver glob of mercury
pulsing in crematorium dust.

5
I've become a handless pilgrim
kneeling to suck up a glossy elver
between my lips, a living yogurt
of morbid hope.   It slips
down into my stomach like the beat
of bad datura getting worse.

6
My hands grow purple buds
and, refusing to touch a clock,
I walk through the charcoal landscape
from Parc Slip to Eglwys Nynnydd
snapping branches from silver,
gold, at last a diamond tree.

CORRUPTED BY BOUNDARIES

Corrupted by boundaries
blotched by rations fifty-seven years ago,
shot with a reach that broke for its prize just
by speckling an empty page. I roam the remains.

My body salts the circle where it is –
from slate to pagoda to adobe roof.

I admit to thoughts I never occupied,
scruples never fully deployed,
vicarious bliss, vicarious crest, flamingos
mottled with a memory of wood anemones.

Now I claim the local and the distant summit,
a portion of Welsh cakes and Carpathian nettles,
moulded to a nautilus doubling its global raid.

All it took was a move from clapping on one hand
to clearing an engine manifold of stars and sand.

NEOLITHIC OAK ROAD

My exit from the Ridgeway furnace
not far from Wayland Smithy –
thorned legs and yet more
triskels wrapped in mine
unlocked from *kama kalpa*,
for a more eclectic remedy.

From Polden Hills, Somerset Levels
cradled all of Glastonbury
with cloud dakini dancers
conquering the sky. An emerald blaze
burned your human face
cadaverous above me. Sinister,

dexterous breasts, bristling with skulls,
return my eyes to the naked sorrow
of approach and then – goodbye
clown nosed sacred gaiety –
shambolic ache of healing songs,
disparate groan of disaffected gongs.

CRIBBWR SEAM

Stooped from the car,
smelled fields around the village.

At the Second Severn Crossing, toll gate
bollards like a sea defense I couldn't breach.

Slurry at home, a bed for my nose
but not the bed predicted.

Give me a stable that smells,
don't lie about the roses.

Steamcoal to the north,
limestone to the south.

Here I sleep among demons,
I couldn't sleep with angels anywhere.

CRAFU SAIM

Ro'n i'n arfer eillio
yn y bath
gan adael cyplysnod o flew
rhanedig
ar ddalen yr enamel gwyn,
fel gorwel o atalnodi
yn crebachu'r cyfoeth
a sgrifennwyd ar wyneb y nos.

Nawr rwy'n byw
ar fy mhen fy hun
rwy'n gybyddlyd â phopeth,
hyd yn oed gwastraff fy nghorff;
heb eillio nac ymolchi
am ddiwrnodau,
ac ôl traed brain
yn wyddor ar groen fy llwch.

Wfft i lendid a threfn –
heb gymorth neb
rwy'n pwyso a mesur pob ystum,
arwyddion blêr annibyniaeth,
gan wybod nad oes neb
yn mynd i ddarllen tomen
y corongylch ond i mi
ei grafu drosof fy hun.

INDEX OF FIRST LINES

 **PS AVALON PUBLISHING**

About PS Avalon

PS Avalon Publishing is an independent and committed publisher offering a complete publishing service. As a small publisher able to take advantage of the latest technological advances, PS Avalon Publishing can offer an alternative route for aspiring authors in our particular fields of interest.

As well as publishing, we offer an education programme including courses, seminars, group retreats, and other opportunities for personal and spiritual growth. Whilst the nature of our work means we engage with people from all around the world, we are based in Glastonbury which is in the West Country of England.

new poetry books

Our purpose is to bring you the best new poetry with a psychospiritual content, work that is contemplative and inspirational, with a dark, challenging edge.

self development books

We publish inspiring reading material aimed at enhancing your personal and spiritual development in which everything is kept as simple and as accessible as possible.

PS AVALON PUBLISHING

Box 1865, Glastonbury,

Somerset BA6 8YR, U.K.

www.willparfitt.com

will@willparfitt.com

Lightning Source UK Ltd.
Milton Keynes UK
UKOW052154251011

180935UK00001B/7/P